CW00555313

How To Ask Great Questions

A Guide to Asking Meaningful and Insightful Questions

Mary J. Greenwood

Copyright © 2023 Mary J. Greenwood

All rights reserved. No portion of this publication may be reproduced, distributed,or transmitted in any form of by any means, including photocopying, recording,or other electronic or mechanical methods, without the prior writing permission of the publisher, except in the case of brief quotations embodied in critical reviews and certain Copyrightothers noncommercial uses permitted by copyright

Table of Contents

Introduction

One of the most fundamental ways we discover more about the world around us is by asking questions. We are naturally intrigued by the sights, sounds, and sensations we encounter from the minute we are born.

As we get older, our queries become more complicated and nuanced as a reflection of our growing world knowledge.

 But not every question is answered equally. While some inquiries are straightforward and superficial, others are profound and perceptive.

While some questions elicit rote, prepared responses, others require in-depth, deliberate thought. Anyone who wants to understand the world more thoroughly and meaningfully must develop their ability to ask great questions. In this manual, we shall examine the craft of asking excellent questions.

We'll look at what constitutes a great inquiry and how to formulate inquiries that generate thoughtful and insightful responses. We'll examine the various question forms and their intended outcomes while also talking about the strategies and tactics you can employ to improve your asking abilities.

In order to demonstrate the value of asking insightful questions, we will use examples from a range of disciplines throughout this manual, including business, philosophy, science, and politics.

We'll examine how important questions have molded our knowledge of the world, stimulated fresh insights, and helped us make sense of the complicated and dynamic environment of contemporary living. This manual will provide you with the skills and knowledge you need to ask insightful questions and unearth fresh insights and knowledge, whether you're a student, researcher, corporate executive, or simply an inquisitive individual looking to enhance your awareness of the world.

So let's set out on this adventure of research and learning and learn how to pose compelling questions that will alter how we perceive the world.

Chapter 1: Why asking great questions matters

Learning to ask excellent questions is one of the most important life skills we can acquire. It allows us to learn new ideas and perspectives, develop a deeper understanding of our surroundings, and engage in meaningful interactions with others.

Whether we are speaking with friends, family, coworkers, or complete strangers, asking intelligent questions can open up a world of possibilities. The foundation of making intelligent queries is curiosity.

It is the desire to learn more, understand things better, and grow as a person. It is the willingness to put our assumptions and beliefs to the test, to look for new information and ideas, and to engage in open dialogue with others. By posing intelligent questions, we invite others to share their knowledge, concepts, and experiences with us and create a space for genuine connection and comprehension. But posing thoughtful questions is not always straightforward.

It demands a readiness to admit our limitations, be vulnerable, and be open to the possibility of being wrong.

Additionally, expertise and training are required. Asking great questions requires active listening, careful thought, contemplation, and the development of thoughtful, engaging, and important inquiries.

Despite the challenges, asking probing questions has many benefits. It can help us make better decisions, build stronger relationships with others, and figure out the meaning and goal of our lives. It can also be a powerful instrument for innovation, creativity, and problem-solving. We challenge ourselves and others to think more critically, investigate innovative ideas, and push the boundaries of what is possible when we ask insightful questions.

In a world that is becoming more complex and interconnected, asking insightful questions has never been more important.

It is the key to learning new things, connecting with others in meaningful ways, and creating a better future for both ourselves and those around us.

Therefore, if you want to maximize your life, expand your knowledge of the world, and effect positive change, start asking excellent questions right away.

A. What makes a question great?

What makes an inquiry incredible is a subject that has been investigated by logicians, teachers, and scholars for quite a long time.

At its center, an incredible inquiry is one that incites thought, advances conversation, and prompts more noteworthy comprehension.

In any case, there are many elements that add to the significance of an inquiry, including its clarity, pertinence, intricacy, and imagination.

One of the main parts of an incredible inquiry is its clarity. A reasonable inquiry is one that is straightforward and has an obvious focus. It ought to be sufficiently explicit to take into consideration an engaged conversation, yet expansive enough to consider alternate points of view and translations.

An unmistakable inquiry likewise assists with guaranteeing that everybody is in total agreement and that the discussion remains focused. Pertinence is one more significant part of an incredible inquiry.

A significant inquiry is one that is opportune and addresses a subject that is significant to the members. It ought to be something that is present in individuals' brains or that can possibly be pertinent to their lives here and there.

At the point when an inquiry is pertinent, it can assist in drawing in individuals and propelling them to partake in the conversation. Intricacy is likewise a vital factor in making an inquiry incredible. A complicated inquiry is one that requires decisive reasoning, reflection, and examination.

It ought to be sufficiently provocative to urge individuals to ponder the subject and investigate alternate points of view and thoughts.

An intricate inquiry can likewise assist with cultivating imagination and development, as individuals are compelled to concoct new and unique perspectives on issues.

An incredible inquiry is, in many cases, an imaginative one.

Inventiveness is the capacity to consider some fresh possibilities and concoct new and imaginative thoughts.

An imaginative inquiry is one that challenges presumptions and urges individuals to think in new and various ways. It ought to be something startling or amazing, and that should pique interest. Notwithstanding these variables, there are a few different characteristics that can add to the significance of an inquiry.

For instance, an incredible inquiry ought to be unassuming, taking into consideration numerous responses and points of view.

It ought to likewise be deferential and comprehensive, keeping away from any language or statement that should have been seen as biased or hostile.

Furthermore, an incredible inquiry ought to be sufficiently adaptable to accommodate different learning styles and correspondence inclinations.

What makes an inquiry incredible is a mix of variables, including lucidity, significance, intricacy, and innovativeness.

At the point when an inquiry is very well created and nicely planned, it has the ability to invigorate conversation, advance comprehension, and move development.

In that capacity, the capacity to pose extraordinary inquiries is a vital expertise for teachers, pioneers, and any individual who looks to take part in significant and useful discussions.

Chapter 2:Understanding the Context.

An extraordinary inquiry is one that invigorates thought, empowers conversation, and at last prompts a more profound comprehension of a specific subject.

Posing extraordinary inquiries is a craft, and dominating this ability can help you in numerous aspects of your life, from building more grounded connections to propelling your vocation.

All in all, what makes an inquiry extraordinary? There are a few critical components to consider:

1. Lucidity: An extraordinary inquiry is clear and straightforward. It ought to be brief and direct, so the individual being asked can rapidly get a handle on what is being requested from them.

Clearness in posing inquiries is vital to really imparting and getting exact data. Whether you are an understudy, specialist, writer, or questioner, posing clear and succinct inquiries is fundamental to accomplishing your ideal result.

 The initial step to achieving clarity in posing inquiries is to comprehend what you need to realize.

This includes having a reasonable idea of what data you want to accumulate and how it will be utilized.
When you have a reasonable comprehension of what you want to be aware of, you can begin figuring out questions that will assist you in

accomplishing your objectives. While clarifying some things, it is essential to be just about as unambiguous as could really be expected.

Ambiguous or general inquiries can prompt obscure or general responses, which may not give you the data you really want.

All things being equal, pose designated inquiries that emphasize the particular data you want to get.

For instance, rather than asking, "What is your viewpoint on this point?", inquire, "Could you at any point give explicit guides to help your perspective on this specific part of the subject?"

Furthermore, it is vital to try not to utilize language or specialized language that may not be perceived by the individual about whom you are inquiring.

Assuming you really want to utilize specialized language, make certain to make sense of any terms or ideas that may not be natural to the individual about whom you are inquiring.

This will guarantee that they can completely comprehend and give exact responses to your inquiries.

One more significant part of lucidity in posing inquiries is to try not to ask leaden or one-sided questions.

Driving inquiries can impact the respondent's response by proposing a specific reaction.

All things being equal, pose unassuming inquiries that permit the individual to give their own reaction without being impacted by your inquiry.

For instance, rather than asking, "Do you suppose this is really smart?", inquire, "What do you honestly think about this thought?"

While getting clarification on some pressing issues, it is critical to effectively pay attention to the reaction and ask follow-up inquiries to explain any data that may not be clear.

This will guarantee that you completely comprehend the data being given and that you can pose extra inquiries that might be fundamental.

Clearness in posing inquiries is fundamental to getting precise and valuable data.

To accomplish lucidity, it is critical to have a reasonable comprehension of what you want to be aware of, pose explicit inquiries, keep away from language and driving inquiries, effectively pay attention to the reaction, and ask follow-up inquiries on a case-by-case basis.

By keeping these rules, you can work on your capacity to really impart and get the data you want.

2. Relevance: An unusual enquiry must be relevant to the topic under consideration. It needs to be intriguing and encourage additional research on the subject.

Posing pertinent questions is a fundamental ability that can help you gather information, communicate your ideas, and solve problems successfully.

Posing the proper questions is essential to achieving your present goals and gaining a deeper understanding of the topic, whether you are in a professional setting, a classroom environment, or a casual talk. Understanding the context of the situation is key when posing important questions. It's important to have a clear understanding of the context, purpose, and goals of the debate before you start asking for clarification on crucial problems.

This might help you formulate your questions in a way that adds value to the dialogue. When asking pertinent questions, it's important to consider the audience you are speaking to.

Because different people possess varying levels of knowledge and skill, asking questions that are either too simple or too complicated may result in confusion or disappointment.

In order to elicit the information you need without overwhelming or disappointing your audience, it is crucial to tailor your inquiries to the level of understanding of the person or group you are speaking to.

Strong listening skills are also necessary when asking crucial questions.

When you're taking part in a discussion, it's important to pay attention to what the other person is saying and to ask follow-up questions that clarify or expand on their points.

This will help you understand the topic more thoroughly and can also demonstrate to the other person that you are genuinely interested in what they have to say.

It's important to ask innocent questions in addition to listening carefully to encourage dialogue and research.

Closed-ended questions that can be answered with a simple "yes" or "no" don't take much research or depth of understanding into account.

If all else is equal, try to ask questions that begin with "how," "why," or "imagine a scenario in which," as these kinds of questions encourage the other person to reflect on the matter and look into alternative viewpoints.

It's crucial to pay attention to the manner in which you phrase your inquiry. Intimidating, harsh, or accusing questions can make the other person uncomfortable and make it harder to have a productive conversation.

All things considered, make an effort to pose questions in a neutral and innocent manner and be receptive to different viewpoints and ideas.

A critical skill that can help you with gaining a deeper understanding of a subject, handling problems, and seriously addressing them with others is asking the right questions. To ask pertinent questions, it's important to understand the context of the situation, cater your questions to your audience, listen attentively and ask follow-up questions, provide unassuming questions that inspire exploration, and be conscious of the tone and expression of your queries.

With these skills, you can improve your communication and problem-solving talents in any situation.

3. Responsiveness: An extraordinary request should be genuine, rather than shut wrapped up.

Questions that could go one way or the other help more low down and clever responses, while shut completed questions can limit the degree of the conversation.

Presenting unprecedented requests is a masterpiece that requires a blend of mastery, creative mind, and straightforwardness. Actually, straightforwardness is perhaps one of the main parts of representing an unprecedented request.

Being open means being willing to tune in, learn, and change as you attempt to gain an ongoing more significant perception of the subject.

Responsiveness in presenting remarkable requests starts with an open viewpoint. You ought to save your inclinations and tendencies and push toward the point with interest and a yearning to learn.

This infers being receptive to weighty contemplations, whether or not they challenge your ongoing convictions or assumptions.

Another piece of responsiveness in presenting remarkable requests is being willing to demand help. No one has all of the reactions, and it's alright to yield when you don't know something. Mentioning clarification or additional information can help you with securing a more significant perception of the subject and lead to extra fast requests.

Additionally, being accessible to substitute perspectives and opinions is imperative for presenting unprecedented requests.

By considering an extent of viewpoints, you can cultivate a more nuanced and careful understanding of the subject.

This can help you with presenting all the more fast and provocative requests that engage further discussion and examination.

Being accessible to info and important analysis is moreover huge.

Presenting extraordinary requests is a communication, and you may not really for each situation hit the bullseye the underlying time. By being accessible to analysis, you can acquire from your blunders and work on your examining skills long term.

responsiveness in presenting exceptional requests incorporates being accessible at that point.

This suggests zeroing in on the singular you're chatting with, really focusing on their responses, and noting carefully.

By being totally present in the conversation, you can cultivate a more significant relationship with the individual and make a more helpful and valuable talk.

Considering everything, straightforwardness is a basic part of presenting unprecedented requests.
By pushing toward the point with an open standpoint, mentioning help, considering substitute perspectives, being accessible to analysis, and being accessible at that point, you can cultivate more cunning and

provocative requests that lead to more significant perception and critical conversations.

4.Sincerity: An extraordinary inquiry ought to come from a position of earnestness and interest. Individuals are bound to answer emphatically to questions that are asked with veritable interest.

Truthfulness is a fundamental part with regards to posing incredible inquiries. Posing inquiries isn't just about social occasion data, yet it's tied in with looking for understanding and explaining contemplations.

To pose extraordinary inquiries, one should be true in their methodology, which includes being certified, genuine, and deferential in their correspondence.

Genuineness is the groundwork of a significant discussion, and laying out trust between the speaker and listener is fundamental.

 At the point when you pose an inquiry, you are basically requesting another person's time and consideration. Consequently, it's critical to be true in your aims and recognize the individual's information, experience, and ability.

To be true in posing extraordinary inquiries, you want to have a current real interest and interest in the subject.

This implies that you ought to pose inquiries for asking, but since you truly need to find out more and gain a more profound comprehension of the subject.

Tell the truth in your communication is additionally significant. This implies being open and straightforward about your goals and the motivation behind your inquiries. Abstain from posing driving inquiries or questions that might have stowed away plans. Your objective ought to be to look for lucidity and understanding, not to control or control the discussion.

One more key part of genuineness in posing extraordinary inquiries is being conscious of the other individual's time and ability.

This implies being patient and mindful of their reactions, giving them sufficient opportunity to think and understand their responses, and trying not to hinder or talk over them.

Conscious correspondence makes a protected and agreeable space for significant discussions and urges the other individual to share their contemplations and experiences.

genuineness is a crucial part in posing extraordinary inquiries. It includes being certifiable, fair, and conscious in your correspondence, showing a veritable interest in the point within reach, and being patient and mindful of the other individual's reactions.

At the point when you approach discussions with genuineness, you make a significant exchange that supports getting the hang of, understanding, and development.

5. Imagination: An incredible inquiry can be inventive or startling. It can move presumptions and lead to new bits of knowledge or thoughts.

Imagination is a fundamental fixing in posing extraordinary inquiries.

It is the capacity to think past the self-evident and to concoct exceptional, provocative requests that can prompt significant and adroit responses. With regards to posing incredible inquiries, innovativeness can have a significant effect between a superficial discussion and a profound investigation of thoughts and points of view.

One method for cultivating imagination in posing extraordinary inquiries is to move toward the subject with a receptive outlook.

It's fundamental to let go of assumptions and suspicions, to investigate additional opportunities and points of view.

This can mean being available to dissimilar thoughts, and not really tolerating the state of affairs as the main way things can be.

One more method for upgrading imagination in posing extraordinary inquiries is to draw from various fields of information and encounters.

Cross-disciplinary reasoning can prompt inventive methodologies and experiences that may not be evident while checking out an issue according to a solitary point of view. By taking into account various perspectives and approaches, one can create a more extensive comprehension of the main thing and pose more educated and keen inquiries.

The utilization of similarities and allegories can likewise be a successful apparatus to encourage imagination in addressing. Similarities and representations can assist

6. Timing: An unprecedented request should be presented splendidly, in the right setting. Representing a request at some unsatisfactory time or in some unsuitable setting can cut down its impact.

Presenting uncommon requests is a mastery that can convey immense worth to your life, whether you're endeavoring to acquire some new valuable information, fostering how you could decipher a subject, or investigating what's going on. Regardless, timing is a fundamental think about presenting staggering requests.

Indeed, it can have the impact between a request that moves information and one that fails spectacularly.

Timing is central since it sets the setting for your request.

If you represent a request at some inadmissible time, it may not be by and large invited, or it may not yield the best result.

The following are a couple of examinations to recall concerning timing in presenting remarkable requests:

a. Contemplate the situation: Different conditions call for different sorts of requests.

For example, in case you're in a social event, it may be more reasonable to represent a request that is relevant to the arrangement, while in a nice conversation, you could have more leeway to present more private or exploratory requests. Contemplate the particular situation and change your examining style similarly.

b. Have some familiarity with the preparation of the conversation: The preparation of your request can influence how it's gotten.

For example, if someone is currently feeling overwhelmed or centered, representing a puzzling or testing request may not be for the most part invited.

Then again, in case someone is in a curious or responsive mindset, they may be more open to exploratory requests.

Center around the up close and personal climate of the conversation and change your examining style likewise.

c. Tune in before you ask: One of the fundamental pieces of timing in presenting unprecedented requests is to tune in before you ask.

By tuning in, you can get a sensation of what's at this point been inspected, what requests have been presented, and what openings or areas of weakness really exist.

This can help you with illustrating your request to such an extent that develops the ongoing conversation, rather than crashing it.

d. Grant time for reflection: Extraordinary requests every now and again anticipate that time should reflect and process.

Expecting that you represent a request that requires a clever reaction, license the other individual opportunity to reflect before expecting a response. This can help with ensuring that the reaction is a lot considered and critical.

e. Show limitation: finally, showing restraint while presenting phenomenal inquiries is basic. Just a single out of each and every odd request will yield a brief reaction or result in a basic comprehension.

Regardless, by presenting sagacious requests dependably for a really long time, you can help with building a culture of solicitation and finding that helps generally closely involved individuals.

timing is an essential work out presenting unprecedented requests.

By considering what's going on, observing the significant climate, tuning in before you ask, allowing time for reflection, and showing restriction, you can present requests that energize information, broaden understanding, and help with pushing conversations ahead in a positive way.

with improving on complex thoughts, and making them more open to other people.

They can likewise start better approaches for thinking, and motivate individuals to see things from an alternate point.

By utilizing similarities and analogies, one can create novel thoughts, and investigate various potential outcomes.

It's likewise fundamental for be interested and curious while posing extraordinary inquiries.

Interest can assist with driving the inventive strategy, as it urges one to investigate novel thoughts, search out new data, and challenge presumptions.

Being curious can likewise assist with creating a more profound comprehension of the main thing, which can prompt more clever inquiries.

Finally, it's fundamental for face challenges while posing incredible inquiries. Imagination includes venturing outside one's usual range of familiarity and investigating new and strange domains.

It very well may be awkward and testing, however facing challenges can likewise prompt creative thoughts and experiences that might not have been imaginable in any case.

imagination is a critical fix in posing extraordinary inquiries.

By moving toward the point with a receptive outlook, drawing from changed fields of information and encounters, utilizing similarities and illustrations, being interested and curious, and being willing to face challenges, one can produce quick and provocative inquiries that can prompt a more profound comprehension of the main

things. With training and commitment, anybody can foster their imaginative reasoning abilities
and become capable in posing extraordinary inquiries.

7. Follow-up: An incredible inquiry ought to prompt further conversation or investigation. Follow-up questions can assist with explaining or develop the first inquiry, prompting a more profound comprehension of the subject.

Posing extraordinary inquiries is an expertise that can be created after some time with training and tolerance.

Nonetheless, posing an extraordinary inquiry is just the most important phase in a bigger course of looking for information and understanding. The subsequent step is to circle back to the inquiry by investigating its suggestions and revealing more data.

One significant part of follow-up is to listen cautiously to the solution to your inquiry. Frequently, the response will give hints to additional inquiries or focuses that should be explained.

By effectively tuning in and drawing in with the individual responding to your inquiry, you can acquire a more profound comprehension of the subject and uncover more bits of knowledge.

One more significant part of follow-up is to be constant in your quest for replies. Extraordinary inquiries frequently lead to complex responses that require further examination or investigation.

It could be important to ask follow-up inquiries or lead examinations to comprehend the ramifications of your underlying inquiry completely. This can include searching out extra wellsprings of data, talking with specialists in the field, or leading your own examinations or examinations.

Furthermore, it is vital to keep a receptive outlook and overhaul your underlying suspicions or theories in light of new data that you reveal through follow-up.

Some of the time, the solution to your underlying inquiry might challenge your current convictions or suppositions, and it is vital to adjust and develop how you might interpret the subject as you find out more.

it is essential to perceive that follow-up is a continuous cycle, and there might very well never be a conclusive response to your underlying inquiry.

Rather, each answer might prompt new inquiries and new roads of investigation, making a ceaseless pattern of request and disclosure.

In synopsis, posing extraordinary inquiries is just the most vital phase in a bigger course of looking for information and understanding.

Follow-up is fundamental to completely investigate the ramifications of your underlying inquiry, uncover new bits of knowledge, and reconsider how you might interpret the subject as you find out more.

By listening cautiously, being tireless, keeping a receptive outlook, and perceiving the continuous idea of the cycle, you can turn into an expert of incredible addressing and keep on extending how you might interpret your general surroundings.

Generally, posing extraordinary inquiries requires a mix of expertise and instinct.

By being clear, significant, open, true, innovative, opportune, and able to follow up, you can turn into an expert at posing extraordinary inquiries. With training, this expertise can assist you with building more grounded connections, gain new experiences, and advance your own and proficient objectives.

A. Know your audience

Understanding your listeners' perspective is fundamental with regards to posing extraordinary inquiries.

Whether you are directing a meeting, giving a show, or participating in a discussion, it is critical to comprehend who your crowd is and what they are keen on.

By understanding your listeners' perspective, you can fit your inquiries to their requirements and interests, making the discussion seriously captivating and useful.

Perhaps the earliest thing to consider while getting to understand what your listeners might be thinking is their experience and level of aptitude.

Assuming you are talking with a gathering of specialists in a specific field, you can pose more itemized and specialized inquiries that will challenge their insight and draw in them in a more profound discussion.

Then again, assuming your crowd is new to the point, vital to pose more broad inquiries will assist them with understanding the rudiments prior to diving further.

One more significant variable to consider while getting to understand what your listeners might be thinking is their inclinations and inspirations.

On the off chance that you can recognize what spurs them, what their objectives are, and what they are energetic about, you can pose inquiries that tap into those interests and make the discussion really captivating.

This can assist construct an association with your crowd and make a more sure and useful environment.

Moreover, it is critical to consider the setting wherein you will pose your inquiries. Is it true or not that you are leading a proper meeting or an easygoing discussion?

Will your crowd be in a loose or high-pressure climate? Understanding the setting in which you will pose your inquiries can assist you with picking the right tone and way of addressing to match what is happening and make the ideal result.

While posing extraordinary inquiries, being clear and succinct in your communication is additionally significant.

Try not to utilize language or specialized terms that your crowd may not comprehend, and make certain to make sense of any mind boggling ideas or thoughts. This can assist your crowd with feeling more good and positive about participating in the discussion, and can likewise assist you with finding more sagacious solutions to your inquiries.

Generally speaking, understanding what your listeners might be thinking is vital to posing incredible inquiries.

By figuring out their experience, interests, inspirations, and the setting wherein you will pose your inquiries, you can fit your inquiries to their requirements and interests, make a positive and connecting with air, and at last accomplish the ideal result of the discussion.

B. Consider the setting

Presenting exceptional requests is an essential mastery that can help you with obtaining further encounters into a particular point, all the more profoundly concentrate on an individual or situation, and finally seek after better decisions.

Regardless, it's crucial to consider the setting wherein you're representing these requests, as this can through and through influence the reactions you get and the general aftereffect of the conversation.

The setting implies the physical and social environment where the conversation occurs.

For example, if you're driving a gathering in a traditional setting, for instance, another worker screening, you'll presumably need to tailor your requests to be more master and coordinated.

Of course, if you're having a casual conversation with colleagues, you could have the choice to present more private or unpretentious requests.

One huge idea while presenting phenomenal requests in any setting is to know about the power components affecting everything.

For example, in case you're conversing with someone for an errand, you hold a particular level of power in the conversation.

This can make the interviewee feel restless or hesitant to share explicit information.

For this present circumstance, it's imperative to present requests to such an extent that consoles the interviewee and urges them to share their contemplations and experiences clearly.

Another huge idea is to be aware of any friendly or typical practices that could impact the conversation.

For example, in specific social orders, it may be considered discourteous to present individual requests, while in others, it very well may be seen as a sign of endlessly interest.

Basically, a couple of subjects may be no or distant in unambiguous gathering conditions, so it's imperative to know about these social nuances while framing your requests.

As a rule, while presenting exceptional requests, it's imperative to consider the setting where you're asking them.

By monitoring the physical and social environment, the power components at play, and any friendly or acknowledged rehearses that could impact the conversation, you can ensure that your requests are by and large invited and lead to huge encounters and conversations. Along these lines, reliably stop briefly to mull over the setting preceding representing your next exceptional request!

C. Identify the purpose of your question

Recognizing the justification behind your request is a basic stage in strong correspondence and information gathering.

It helps you with illustrating your solicitation in a way that is clear, brief, and relevant to the ongoing situation.

Understanding the inspiration driving your request can similarly help you with choosing the most fitting person to ask, the most obvious opportunity to ask, and the level of detail expected in the response.

One of the basic clarifications behind distinctive the justification for your request is to ensure that you are representing the right request.

Every now and again, we present requests that are not relevant to the situation or that are unreasonably large to give us the specific information we need.

By tracking down an open door to make sense of the inspiration driving our request, we can do whatever it takes not to present unessential or ineffective requests.

Another inspiration to recognize the justification behind your request is to ensure that you are asking it in a way that is cognizant and fitting.

Different conditions could require different sorts of requests, and indispensable to present requests are legitimate for the special circumstance.

For example, if you are representing a singular request, it may be more legitimate to ask in a one-on-one conversation rather than in a public setting.

Perceiving the inspiration driving your request can similarly help you with choosing the best person to ask.

Accepting you are looking for particular information, you could need to ask someone with ability around there.

If you are looking for day to day consolation, you could need to ask a buddy or relative who is a good crowd.

By recognizing the justification for your request, you can ensure that you are requesting that the ideal individual finish everything.

perceiving the justification behind your request can help you with concluding the level of detail expected in the response.

If you are looking for a general framework, you may not need a point by point response.

In any case, if you truly need unequivocal information, you could need to present more point by point and express requests.

By perceiving the justification behind your request, you can ensure that you are mentioning the legitimate level of detail.

perceiving the justification behind your request is a principal stage in strong correspondence and information gathering.

It can help you with representing the right request, ask it in a reasonable way, ask the ideal individual, and earn the college education of detail you need.

Via cutting out an open door to make sense of the justification behind your request, you can ensure that your solicitation is fruitful and helpful.

Chapter 3: Types of Questions

Questions assume a basic part in correspondence, as they assist people with social event data, express interest, and fabricate connections.

There are a few kinds of inquiries, and understanding them can assist people with imparting all the more successfully in different settings, including individual and expert settings.

In this article, we will examine the absolute most normal kinds of inquiries.

understanding the various kinds of inquiries can assist people with conveying all the more successfully in many settings. By involving the suitable kind of inquiry for a specific circumstance, people can assemble data, construct connections, and work with additional significant discussions.

The following are a few sorts of inquiries

A. Open-finished questions

They are intended to energize a more definite, top to bottom reaction. They permit people to offer their viewpoints, sentiments, and suppositions, and frequently start with words, for example, "what," "how," "why," or "fill me in about."

Instances of unassuming inquiries incorporate "What is your take on this present circumstance?" "What was your opinion about the show?" and "Educate me regarding your experience."

Unassuming inquiries are questions that can't be responded to with a basic "yes" or "no" reaction.

They are intended to evoke point by point, interesting reactions from the individual being inquired. Unassuming inquiries can be utilized in various settings, including meetings, reviews, and discussions.

One of the advantages of utilizing inquiries without a right or wrong answer is that they consider a more top to bottom investigation of a subject or issue.

Rather than restricting the discussion to a thin arrangement of reactions, questions that could go either way urge the speaker to share their considerations, sentiments, and encounters.

This can prompt a more profound comprehension of a theme and can assist with revealing new experiences and points of view.

Unassuming inquiries additionally have the advantage of being more captivating for the individual being inquired. Since they require more thought and reflection to reply, they can assist with making a more significant and vital experience for the speaker. This can be particularly significant in circumstances where you are attempting to construct compatibility or lay out an association with somebody.

Instances of inquiries without a right or wrong answer include:

What is your take on the ongoing political environment?

How might you depict your optimal workplace?

What difficulties have you faced in your own life, and how have you conquered them?

What are probably the main illustrations you have learned in your profession?

What persuades you to continue to push advance, in any event, when circumstances become difficult?

While utilizing inquiries without a right or wrong answer, it is critical to recall that they ought to be utilized in a manner that is deferential and non-critical.

Abstain from posing driving inquiries that steer the discussion in a specific heading, and be mindful so as not to make suspicions or decisions about the speaker's reactions.

 questions that could go either way are an amazing asset for making significant and connecting discussions.

Whether you are directing a meeting, looking over clients, or basically attempting to get to realize somebody better, they can assist with encouraging further associations and open important bits of knowledge.

B. Shut finished questions

Shut finished questions require a short, explicit response. They are frequently used to get real data or affirm a specific point. These inquiries commonly start with expressions, for example, "yes" or "no," "do you," or "is it." Instances of shut finished questions incorporate

"Do you like pizza?" "Would you say you are coming to the party this evening?" and "Is the gathering at 3 pm?"

Shut finished questions will be questions that can be responded to with a basic "yes" or "no," or a particular response that falls inside a bunch of foreordained choices.

They are many times utilized in overviews, interviews, and different types of exploration to gather quantitative information and to evoke explicit data from respondents.

One of the primary benefits of shut finished questions is that they are not difficult to examine and measure.

Since the responses are restricted to a bunch of foreordained choices, they can be effectively counted and examined to recognize patterns and examples in the information.

Shut finished questions are additionally helpful when specialists need to think about reactions across various gatherings or when they need to follow changes in reactions over the long run.

One more benefit of shut finished questions is that they are not difficult to direct.

Respondents don't have to invest a ton of energy pondering their responses or planning a reaction, which makes them bound to finish the study or interview. This is especially significant while leading exploration with enormous gatherings or when time is restricted.

Nonetheless, there are likewise a few burdens to utilizing shut finished questions.

One of the fundamental determinants is that they can restrict the profundity of the reaction.

Since respondents are restricted to a bunch of foreordained choices, they will most likely be unable to completely offer their viewpoints and sentiments on a specific subject.
This can be especially risky when scientists are attempting to investigate complex issues or when they need to figure out the subtleties of a specific point.

One more hindrance of shut finished questions is that they can be one-sided. Scientists may accidentally incorporate choices that are better to one reaction over another, which can slant the aftereffects of the review.

For instance, assuming that a review question finds out if they concur or contradict a specific assertion, the choices gave might be phrased such that favors understanding over conflict.

 shut finished questions are a helpful device for gathering quantitative information and inspiring explicit data from respondents.

They are not difficult to control and investigate, yet they can likewise restrict the profundity of the reaction and be one-sided.

While utilizing shut finished questions, scientists actually must cautiously consider the choices gave and to guarantee that they are not unintentionally affecting the reactions of their members.

C. Probing questions

Testing questions are utilized to acquire further explanation or comprehension of a point or circumstance.

These inquiries are much of the time used to accumulate more data, challenge suppositions, or investigate thoughts in more profundity.

Instances of examining questions incorporate "Could you at any point make sense of that in more detail?"

"For what reason do you imagine that is the situation?" and "What different choices have you thought of?"

Testing questions are a fundamental instrument for social event data and acquiring further experiences into a specific theme or circumstance.

These sorts of inquiries are intended to urge the respondent to develop their underlying response and give more itemized and nuanced reactions.

Testing questions can be utilized in various settings, from meetings to concentrate gatherings to regular discussions, to evoke a more profound comprehension of a theme.

Testing questions can take many structures, yet they all offer the shared objective of empowering the respondent to give more data.

Questions that could go either way, which consider a large number of reactions, are in many cases utilized as examining questions. For instance, rather than posing a yes or no inquiry like "Did you partake in the film?" an examining question may be "What was your take of the film?"

This sort of inquiry permits the respondent to give a more definite reaction and to expound on their viewpoints and sentiments about the film.

One more typical sort of testing question is a subsequent inquiry.

This kind of inquiry is utilized to explain or develop a past reaction.

For instance, assuming somebody makes reference to that they struggled in school, a subsequent testing question may be "Might you at any point enlighten me seriously concerning that?

What explicitly made it hard for you?" This kind of inquiry urges the respondent to give more data about their experience and can assist the questioner or conversationalist with acquiring a more profound comprehension of the circumstance.

Examining questions are additionally valuable for investigating alternate points of view and uncovering fundamental inspirations.

For instance, on the off chance that somebody offers areas of strength for a specific issue, a testing question may be

"What encounters or convictions drove you to shape that assessment?"

This kind of inquiry urges the respondent to consider their own convictions and values and can assist the questioner or conversationalist with acquiring a superior comprehension of the hidden explanations behind their viewpoint.

One of the main abilities for utilizing testing questions really is undivided attention.

Testing questions require the questioner or conversationalist to give close consideration to the respondent's underlying responses and to utilize that data to direct subsequent inquiries.

Undivided attention includes hearing what the respondent is talking about, yet additionally focusing on their manner of speaking, non-verbal communication, and other nonverbal signs.

By being completely present and taking part in the discussion, the questioner or conversationalist can utilize examining inquiries to assemble more definite and nuanced data.

Testing questions are a fundamental instrument for acquiring further bits of knowledge into a specific theme or circumstance. By utilizing genuine inquiries, follow-up questions, and different sorts of testing questions, questioners and conversationalists can urge respondents to give more definite and nuanced reactions.

Undivided attention is a critical expertise for utilizing examining questions successfully, as it permits the questioner or conversationalist to assemble data from the respondent's words, yet in addition their nonverbal signals.

With training, anybody can foster the abilities expected to utilize testing questions actually and gain further experiences into individuals and circumstances around them.

D. Leading questions:

Driving inquiries are intended to guide or impact the reaction of the individual being addressed.

They frequently contain presumptions or propose a specific response. Driving inquiries can be utilized to impact assessments or convictions, and they are frequently viewed as manipulative.

Instances of driving inquiries incorporate "Wouldn't you say this is smart?" "Couldn't you concur that this is the best strategy?" and "You don't actually trust that, isn't that right?"

Driving inquiries are a sort of inquiry that unobtrusively recommend a specific response or impact the respondent's perspective.

These sorts of inquiries are many times utilized in studies, interviews, and legal actions to get data that the examiner wants.

Driving inquiries can be dangerous in light of the fact that they might bring about one-sided or wrong reactions and can influence the validity of the data gathered.

In this note, we will talk about the qualities of driving inquiries, the issues they can cause, and systems to try not to utilize them.

Qualities of Driving Inquiries:

Driving inquiries are generally described by the accompanying attributes:

a. Intriguing: They propose a specific reaction or a specific perspective.

b. One-sided: They contain components that might lead the respondent to reply with a certain goal in mind.

c. Hypothetical: They expect specific realities or viewpoints that may not be precise.

d. Manipulative: They plan to control or impact the respondent's perspective or perspective.

Instances of Driving Inquiries:

Instances of driving inquiries can incorporate the accompanying:

Wouldn't you say that this new approach will take care of our concerns?

Isn't it genuine that you were engaged with the occurrence?

Could you concur that our item is awesome available?

Wouldn't you say it's out of line that you were not given an advancement?

Issues Brought up by Driving Doubts:

The utilization of driving inquiries can bring about various issues:

One-sided reactions: Driving inquiries can impact the respondent's response and result in a one-sided reaction.

a. inaccurate data: The data gathered through driving inquiries may not be exact, as it could be founded on suppositions or controlled conclusions.

b Validity issues: The utilization of driving inquiries can harm the validity of the data gathered and may go with it hard to use in choice making processes.

c .Moral worries: The utilization of driving inquiries can raise moral worries, especially in legal actions, where the objective is to get exact and honest data.

Procedures to Abstain from Utilizing Driving Inquiries:

To abstain from utilizing driving inquiries, following these strategies is significant:

a. Be impartial: Questions ought to be unbiased and not propose a specific response.

b. Keep away from presumptions: Questions shouldn't expect specific realities or viewpoints.

c. Utilize unassuming inquiries: Questions ought to be unconditional and permit the respondent to give their own response.

d. Stay away from stacked terms: Questions ought to try not to utilize terms that are stacked with importance, for example, "out of line" or "best.

Driving inquiries can be hazardous on the grounds that they might bring about one-sided or mistaken reactions, harm the validity of the data gathered, and raise moral worries.

It is critical to abstain from utilizing driving inquiries by following techniques, for example, being unbiased, keeping away from suspicions, utilizing questions that could go either way, and staying away from stacked terms.

By following these techniques, the data gathered will be more precise and trustworthy, and dynamic cycles can be more viable.

E. Hypothetical questions

are used to examine speculative conditions or circumstances.

They much of the time start with articulations, for instance, "envision a situation where" or "expect to be that." These requests can be significant for conceptualizing, decisive reasoning, or exploring potential outcomes.

Cases of speculative requests consolidate "Envision a situation in which we duplicated our advancing spending plan?"

"Expect we introduced another item offering, what could happen?" and "How should you answer if you scored that sweepstakes."

Theoretical requests are a sort of solicitation that incorporate imagining what is going on or situation and asking what could happen or how someone would reply.

These requests as often as possible begin with phrases like "envision a situation where" or "expect to be that" and are normally used in different settings, including conversations, gatherings, and tests.

One of the chief benefits of speculative requests is that they can help people think innovatively and on a very basic level about a given situation.

By addressing what is happening, individuals are constrained to contemplate various expected results and potential outcomes, and to imagine how they could reply in different circumstances.

This can be particularly significant in decisive reasoning settings, as it urges individuals to explore an extent of potential game plans and to mull over the implications of their decisions.

Speculative requests can similarly be used to energize discussion and conversation, particularly in researcher and academic settings.
By mentioning that individuals consider hypothetical circumstances, educators and researchers can encourage them to examine different viewpoints and to attract complex contemplations and thoughts.

This can help individuals with cultivating their conclusive thinking skills, and to end up being all the more okay with unclearness and weakness.

Regardless, it is crucial for observe that there are a couple of limitations to the usage of speculative requests.

For example, now and again, theoretical circumstances may be unnecessarily irrational or unreasonable to be important. Besides, a couple of individuals could fight to think imaginatively or may find hypothetical requests perplexing or overwhelming.

Analysts ought to be fragile to these factors and to moreover tailor their investigating approach.

speculative requests can be a mind boggling resource for engaging imaginativeness, definitive thinking, and discussion.

By mentioning that individuals ponder hypothetical circumstances and to imagine how they could reply, analysts can help with developing further responsibility and understanding, and to encourage individuals to mull over complex issues and thoughts.

F. Rhetorical questions

Facetious inquiries are intended to come to a meaningful conclusion or make an effect, instead of to get a reaction.

These inquiries are much of the time utilized in discourses or introductions to draw in the crowd and urge them to ponder a specific point or issue.

Instances of facetious inquiries incorporate "Could we at any point truly bear to stand by any more?" "Isn't it time we made a move?" and "Do we truly need to go down this way?"

Non-serious inquiries are an amazing asset in correspondence that can be utilized to enthrall a crowd of people and draw in them in a discussion.

A non-serious inquiry is an inquiry that is posed for impact or accentuation and doesn't need a response.

It is an approach to saying something through an inquiry, which can assist with convincing, illuminating or challenging the audience.

Facetious inquiries are utilized in various settings, including discourses, discussions, papers, and regular discussions.

They can be utilized to cause to notice a point, to underline a specific thought, or to urge the audience to ponder a subject.

 They are frequently used to make a feeling of show, pressure, or tension, and can be a powerful approach to keeping the audience locked in.

One of the advantages of facetious inquiries is that they can be utilized to direct the audience towards a specific end.

By suggesting a conversation starter that drives the audience towards a particular response, the speaker has some control over the bearing of the discussion and the way that the audience sees the subject.

This can be especially helpful in powerful discourses or discussions, where the speaker is attempting to persuade the crowd of a specific perspective.

Non-serious inquiries can likewise be utilized to challenge the audience's suppositions or convictions.

By posing an inquiry that powers the audience to reevaluate their situation, the speaker can urge them to ponder a point and to investigate alternate points of view.

This can be a helpful strategy in scholastic composition, where the essayist is attempting to challenge existing speculations or thoughts.

Be that as it may, it is vital to utilize facetious inquiries cautiously, as they can likewise be seen as manipulative or disparaging whenever abused.

It is vital to find some kind of harmony between connecting with the audience and regarding their knowledge and independence.

Non-serious inquiries ought to be utilized sparingly, and just when they are suitable and compelling with regards to the discussion.

non-serious inquiries are a significant device in correspondence that can be utilized to connect with a group of people, guide the discussion, and challenge presumptions.

They can be utilized to convince, illuminate or challenge the audience, and are especially powerful in enticing talks or discussions.

In any case, they ought to be utilized cautiously and sparingly, and ought to continuously regard the knowledge and independence of the audience.

Chapter 4 : Asking Effective Questions

Posing successful inquiries is a pivotal expertise that can assist you with social occasion data, gain experiences, and develop how you might interpret a point or circumstance.

Whether you are an understudy, an expert, or an inquisitive individual, excelling at posing great inquiries can fundamentally improve your learning, critical thinking, and correspondence capacities.

The initial step to posing successful inquiries is to approach them obviously and definitively.

You ought to start by distinguishing the reason for your request and the extent of the data you want. This can include separating complex ideas into less difficult parts, characterizing key terms, and explaining any presumptions or predispositions that might impact your reasoning.

When you have a reasonable thought of what you need to ask, you ought to think about the specific circumstance and crowd of your request.

This can incorporate factors, for example, the degree of information and aptitude of the individual you are asking, the idea of the topic, and the social and normal practices that might influence correspondence.

Fitting your inquiries to these elements can assist you with inspiring more useful and applicable reactions.

One more significant part of posing successful inquiries is to listen effectively and mindfully to the responses. This includes hearing the words as well as grasping the fundamental significance and plan behind them.

By utilizing follow-up questions, rewording, and summing up, you can explain any uncertainty, affirm your comprehension, and develop the discussion.

Additionally, it is vital for be receptive and non-critical while getting clarification on some things.

This implies keeping away from suspicions, generalizations, or predispositions that might incline your reasoning and break your capacity to learn.

All things considered, you ought to move toward every request with interest, modesty, and an eagerness to challenge your own convictions and presumptions.

posing successful inquiries is a fundamental expertise that requires clearness, setting mindfulness, undivided attention, and liberality. By leveling up this ability, you can improve your learning, critical thinking, and correspondence capacities and gain a more profound comprehension of your general surroundings.

A. Start with why

Maybe the principal rule in any endeavor, be it individual or master, is to start with the request "why?"

Understanding the major explanation or motivation driving any task or decision is basic to gaining ground and fulfilling your targets continually.

The power of starting with why ought to be noticeable in different settings.

For example, in business, an association that is clear about its inspiration and values will undoubtedly attract and hold clients, laborers, and monetary sponsors who share those comparable convictions.

By giving the "why" behind their things or organizations, associations can make a more significant relationship with their accomplices and develop a more steadfast following.

In like manner, in confidential life, starting with why can help us with making better decisions and continue with extra conscious lives.

By understanding our secret motivations and values, we can change our exercises to our goals and seek after choices that are as per our genuine selves.

In any case, starting with why isn't straightforward constantly.

It requires a status to challenge assumptions and dive further into our own convictions and motivations.

It will in general be off-kilter to go facing our own tendencies and predispositions, yet doing so is essential to really grasp ourselves as well as others.

starting with why there are areas of strength that can help us with gaining ground and fulfillment in all pieces of our lives.

By representing the request "why" and hoping to grasp our own motivations and values, we can make an all the more clear internal compass and heading, develop more grounded associations, and go with better decisions.

So at whatever point you're defied with a decision or task, try in any case why and see where it takes you.

B. Use clear and concise language

It is crucial to use concise, precise language when seeking clarification on urgent matters to ensure that the intended message is accurately conveyed.

The way you phrase your question can have a significant impact on the response you receive, whether you're asking in a professional or private situation.

First and foremost, using clear language means using phrases that are easily understood by the person you are asking.

Avoid using technical or confusing jargon that the audience or reader might not be familiar with. If your enquiry calls for a specific term or concept, try to define it in clear terms before moving on.

Furthermore, using concise language is important when asking compelling questions.

This entails being prompt and direct, without providing extra information or confusing your message.

Avoid using long or complicated sentences that can cause the audience or reader to lose sight of the question being asked.

Keep in mind that a brief question can frequently elicit a more useful and persuasive response.

While seeking clarification on urgent matters, it is also crucial to take into account the particular situation and tone where the inquiry is being posed.

For instance, using a polite and aware tone will help you gain a favorable response on the odd chance that you are asking for assistance or an explanation. Basically, using more conventional language and structure may be necessary if you are asking a question in a professional setting.

It's important to use concise, precise language when asking questions to ensure effective communication.

You can increase your chances of receiving a reasonable and encouraging response by using easily understood language, avoiding irrelevant information, and considering the particular situation and tone of the enquiry.

C. Avoid assumptions

Questioning is a crucial component of communication, but it's important to do so with consideration and care.

Assumptions are among the most frequent errors people make when asking questions. Assuming anything about the individual, circumstance, or subject you are inquiring about can result in misunderstandings.

Making assumptions puts you at risk of painting a skewed and unreliable picture of what is actually taking place.

This may result in misconceptions and misinterpretations, which can be detrimental to interpersonal relationships on both a personal and professional level.

For instance, you might cause unneeded tension or harm the connection if you make a query out of the presumption that someone is upset with you.

As a result, it's critical to steer clear of assumptions as much as possible when answering questions.

Being open-minded and wanting to learn more about each subject is a good strategy to avoid making assumptions.

Take the time to acquire information and seek clarity rather than thinking you already know the solution or the circumstances.

This can be done by following up with inquiries, paying close attention to the other person's response, and being prepared to acknowledge ignorance.

Using neutral language in your inquiries is another effective method for avoiding assumptions.

This entails staying away from queries that seem predisposed to a particular solution or viewpoint.

Instead, make an effort to ask open-ended questions that let the respondent speak freely without fear of criticism or pressure.

Finally, it's critical to understand how assumptions can become ingrained in our attitudes and actions.

So, when asking questions, it might be beneficial to practice mindfulness and self-awareness.

Before you ask a question, take a moment to consider your own preconceptions and biases.

Then, resolve to approach each interaction with an open and inquisitive mind.

In conclusion, it is crucial for effective communication and developing good connections to refrain from making assumptions when you are asking questions.

You can have a more accurate and meaningful conversation with others if you approach each question with an open mind, speak in an impartial manner, and engage in mindfulness and self-awareness exercises.

D. Ask one question at a time

It is easier for the other person to grasp what you are asking for and to reply appropriately when you ask one question at a time.

This enables a more concentrated discourse that is more fruitful and may produce better results.

On the other hand, asking several questions at once might be confusing and make it challenging for the other individual to give an accurate response.

A more thorough response can be obtained if you ask one question at a time.

When you ask several questions at once, the respondent might just address the most urgent of them, leaving other crucial inquiries unanswered. This may result in miscommunication and inaccurate information.

One question at a time also shows that you value the other person's time and attention.

Someone may perceive it as intrusive or impolite if you ask them a lot of questions all at once.

One inquiry at a time demonstrates that you respect their time and are ready to hear their response.

One key communication technique that can enhance the efficiency of your talks is asking one question at a time.

It enables deeper comprehension, more thorough responses, and demonstrates consideration for the other person's time and attention. Therefore, for a more efficient and fruitful conversation, keep in mind to ask one question at a time the next time you're conversing.

E. Listen actively

The critical ability of active listening is necessary for effective communication. When there are questions involved, active listening becomes much more crucial.

Active listening is when you give the speaker your whole attention and make an effort to understand what they are saying.

It requires paying close attention to the verbal and nonverbal clues of the speaker.

Actively listening while posing questions can aid in your understanding of the speaker's perspective.

It allows you the chance to ask more thought-provoking and pertinent questions and demonstrates to the speaker your appreciation for their point of view.

Here are some guidelines for asking questions while actively listening: Be there: Make sure you are entirely in the moment when you inquire.

Avoid getting distracted by activities like checking your phone or making plans for the future.

Give the speaker your whole attention and listen to what they have to say.

a. Concentrate to comprehend: To better understand the speaker's message, you should ask questions. To achieve this, you must listen to understand rather than to respond.

Don't interrupt or finish the speaker's phrases for them.

Paraphrase what the speaker stated to demonstrate that you understand what they were attempting to communicate after they are finished speaking. Then, restate the main points to make sure you understand the message. Pose queries that can be answered in more than one way, such as "yes" or "no."

b. Instead, use open-ended inquiries to compel the speaker to articulate their thoughts.
  To demonstrate that you are listening to what the speaker is saying, use nonverbal cues.

Nodding your head, maintaining eye contact, and bending forward are some examples. Active listening is a prerequisite for questioning.

Make sure you are totally present in the conversation; listen to understand, paraphrase, and summarize; ask open-ended questions; and use nonverbal clues when you are actively listening. It enables you to comprehend the speaker's message more thoroughly, ask more intelligent questions, and show that you respect their viewpoint. Active listening can help you improve your communication abilities and develop stronger relationships with others.

Chapter Five: Tips for Asking Great Questions

A key technique for self-improvement, personal growth, and learning is asking insightful questions.

Knowing how to ask excellent questions may make a huge impact, whether you're a student, a professional, or just someone who wants to better comprehend the world.

I'll give some advice on how to ask excellent questions in this letter.

A. Be curious

Incredible inquiries are explicit, centered, and clear. Stay away from ambiguous or excessively expensive inquiries, as they are less inclined to yield significant responses.

All things considered, attempt to be basically as unambiguous as conceivable in your inquiries.

This will assist you with getting the data you really want and help other people comprehend what you are inquiring.

Posing inquiries is a significant piece of correspondence. It permits us to explain our grasping, accumulate data, and gain bits of knowledge into a subject or circumstance.

In any case, the nature of the responses we get is not set in stone by the nature of the inquiries we pose. To this end it is pivotal to be explicit while seeking clarification on some things.

Being explicit means posing inquiries that are clear, compact, and centered.

It implies keeping away from obscure or questionable language and being just about as exact as could really be expected.

At the point when you pose explicit inquiries, you are bound to find explicit solutions that furnish you with the data you want.

Here are a few methods for being explicit while seeking clarification on some things:

a. Utilize clear and compact language. Try not to utilize language or specialized terms that may not be perceived by everybody.

b..Be zeroed in on the subject in question. Try not to pose wide or general inquiries that are hard to reply. All things being equal, pose explicit inquiries that relate straightforwardly to the issue you are attempting to address.

c. Utilize inquiries without a right or wrong answer.

Questions that could go either way empower conversation and permit the individual you are talking with to give more definite responses.

d. Try not to lead questions. Driving inquiries can inclination the responses you get, so attempt to keep your inquiries nonpartisan and impartial.

e. Utilized follow-up questions.
On the off chance that you don't comprehend the response you get, or on the other hand assuming you really want more data, make it a point to ask follow-up inquiries. This can assist with explaining any

disarray and guarantee that you have a reasonable comprehension of the point.

By being explicit while getting clarification on pressing issues, you can further develop your relational abilities and assemble the data you really want to pursue informed choices.

Whether you are directing a meeting, going to a gathering, or basically having a discussion with somebody, being explicit can assist you with benefiting from your collaborations.

So the following time you have an inquiry to pose, pause for a minute to contemplate how you can be essentially as unambiguous as could be expected.

C. Be open-minded

Posing extraordinary inquiries requires a receptive outlook.

Stand by listening to alternate points of view, think about novel thoughts, and challenge your own presumptions.

At the point when you approach inquiries with a receptive outlook, you are bound to uncover new experiences and gain from others.

Being liberal is a characteristic that can be unquestionably important in both individual and expert settings.

At the point when you're receptive, you're willing to think about groundbreaking thoughts, viewpoints, and approaches that might be unique in relation to your own. This can prompt development and learning, as well as expanded joint effort and understanding.

At its center, being liberal is tied in with embracing variety.

Whether it's variety in thought, foundation, or culture, being liberal means recognizing that there are various perspectives and living, and that everyone has its own worth.

By freeing yourself up to these alternate points of view, you can widen your comprehension and might interpret the world and become more sympathetic and empathetic towards others.

Being liberal can likewise be unimaginably valuable in critical thinking.

At the point when you're confronted with a troublesome test, it's not difficult to stall out in your own reasoning and battle to concoct new arrangements.

However, when you're liberal, you're ready to take a gander at the issue from various points and think about a more extensive scope of conceivable outcomes.

This can assist you with seeing additional inventive and successful arrangements that you might not have in any case thought of.

Obviously, being liberal isn't simple all the time.

It may very well be challenging to relinquish your own assumptions and inclinations, and to pay attention to and consider the points of view of others genuinely

. In any case, the advantages of being receptive merit the work. By embracing variety and taking into account groundbreaking thoughts, you can develop personally and extend your viewpoints in manners you might very well never have envisioned.

being liberal is an important characteristic that can prompt individual and expert development.

By embracing variety and taking into account new viewpoints, you can turn into a more compassionate, imaginative, and compelling issue solver. While it may not generally be simple, the advantages of being receptive are certainly worth the work.

D. Be respectful

Posing incredible inquiries is a significant expertise that can assist you with looking further into the world, grow your insight, and fabricate better associations with others.

Nonetheless, it's essential that the way in which you pose inquiries is similarly all around as significant as what you inquire.

Being aware and chivalrous in your scrutinizing can assist you with building trust and compatibility with others, stay away from misconceptions, and cultivate useful discussions.

One critical part of deferential addressing is to move toward the individual you're addressing with a receptive outlook and certifiable interest. Try not to make suspicions or decisions about their reactions, and on second thought center around listening cautiously and attempting to grasp their viewpoint.

This implies trying not to stack or lead questions that recommend a specific response, as well as questions that might seem to be fierce or forceful.

One more significant variable to remember is to know about the specific situation and timing of your inquiries.

Contingent upon the circumstance, certain inquiries might be improper or heartless.

For instance, getting some information about their own life or convictions in an expert setting may not be proper, while getting some information about their encounters with psychological wellness might be more fitting in a private and strong setting.

It's additionally vital to be aware of your tone and non-verbal communication while getting clarification on pressing issues.

Abstain from appearing to be pushy, requesting, or pompous, as this can make the other individual become guarded or closed down.

All things considered, move toward your inquiries with a certifiable interest and regard for the other individual's considerations and sentiments.

In conclusion, be ready to listen effectively and participate in a significant discussion.

This implies focusing on the other individual's reactions, asking follow-up inquiries, and being willing to think about alternate points of view.

Recall that posing extraordinary inquiries isn't just about finding solutions, yet in addition about building further associations and understanding with others.

Being conscious while posing extraordinary inquiries is a basic expertise that can assist you cultivate better connections and correspondence with others.

By moving toward your inquiries with a receptive outlook, consciousness of setting and timing, and a veritable interest in others, you can construct trust, keep away from misconceptions, and take part in useful discussions that benefit all interested parties.

Incredible inquiries are conscious. Be aware of individuals you are posing inquiries to, and keep away from questions that are inconsiderate, coldhearted, or improper.

Recognize their insight and mastery, and casing your inquiries in a way that is well mannered and obliging.

E. Use follow-up questions

Incredible inquiries frequently lead to additional inquiries.

Use follow-up inquiries to jump further into a subject and reveal more bits of knowledge.

Follow-up questions can assist with explaining any disarray, give additional background info, and urge others to share their considerations and thoughts.

Posing incredible inquiries is a significant ability for compelling correspondence and critical thinking. In any case, just posing an inquiry isn't sufficient to get significant reactions.
   It is similarly vital to utilize follow-up inquiries to explain and extend the discussion.

Follow-up questions are intended to dig further into the current point, accumulate more data, and show that you are effectively participating in the discussion.

They are especially helpful for complex subjects or while managing people who might be hesitant to share their contemplations and sentiments.

While asking follow-up inquiries, essential to keep away from shut finished questions can be responded to with a basic "yes" or "no."

All things considered, utilize questions that could go either way that urge the other individual to expand and give more detail.

For instance, rather than inquiring "Did you partake in the gathering?" inquire "What did you see as most important about the meeting?"

One more significant part of asking follow-up inquiries is to pay attention to the next individual's reactions effectively.

Focus on their manner of speaking, non-verbal communication, and nonverbal signs.

This won't just assist you with grasping their point of view yet additionally show that you esteem their feedback.

Some successful subsequent inquiries include:

Might you at any point enlighten me

seriously concerning that?

How did that cause you to feel?

What do you figure made that occur?

Might you at any point give me a model?

What might happen if...?

Utilizing follow-up questions further develops correspondence and understanding as well as assists fabricate affinity and entrust with others.

It shows that you are truly intrigued by what they need to say and are focused on cooperating to track down arrangements.

While posing incredible inquiries is a significant ability, utilizing follow-up questions is similarly vital to get significant reactions, assemble more data, and extend the discussion.

By effectively tuning in and utilizing genuine inquiries, you can construct better connections and pursue more educated choices.

F. Practice active listening

Active listening is necessary for asking outstanding questions.

Pay close attention to the responses you get, and utilize what you discover to inform your follow-up inquiries.

You can improve your connections with others, gain a deeper understanding of a subject, and facilitate more meaningful conversations by actively listening.

Whether you are in a personal or professional context, active listening and asking insightful questions are two crucial abilities that go hand in hand.

Active listening is being fully present and involved in a conversation, and asking insightful questions promotes more clarity, better knowledge, and stronger connections with people.

Start by paying close attention to the speaker in order to improve your listening and questioning skills.

This entails putting down any distractions, such as your phone or computer, making eye contact with the speaker, and paying attention to what they have to say.

Avoid interrupting or planning your next words because doing so can make it difficult for you to completely comprehend what is being said.

Pay attention to the speaker's words as well as their meaning while you listen.

Keep an eye out for any nonverbal indicators, such as body language or facial expressions, as these can provide crucial context to the speaker's message.

Strive to ask open-ended questions that promote more in-depth reflection and discussion rather than simple, one-sided ones when it comes to asking great questions.

For instance, you may question "What was the most interesting or challenging part of your day?" instead of "What did you do today?"

This kind of query invites the speaker to elaborate on their experiences, which might result in a deeper exchange of ideas.

Being inquisitive and sincerely interested in the speaker's viewpoint are important components of asking excellent questions.
Stay away from asking judgmental or questions that imply you already know the

answer. Instead, enter the discussion with an open mind and the desire to learn.

You may strengthen your connections with others, learn new things, and improve your understanding of the world around you by engaging in active listening and asking insightful questions.

You can master both of these crucial abilities with time and effort, but it needs practice and focus.

G. Keep an open mind

Posing extraordinary inquiries requires a receptive outlook. Stand by listening to alternate points of view, think about novel thoughts, and challenge your own suspicions.

At the point when you approach inquiries with a receptive outlook, you are bound to reveal new experiences and gain from others.

Posing inquiries is a fundamental part of learning and self-improvement.

Whether you're attempting to extend your insight, resolve an issue, or comprehend another idea, posing inquiries can assist you with finding the solutions you really want.

Notwithstanding, it's fundamental to keep a receptive outlook while posing inquiries to guarantee that you get precise and important data.

At the point when you pose an inquiry, it's vital that you're looking for data, not approval of your current convictions or sentiments.
On the off chance that you approach an inquiry with a shut brain, you might pass up significant bits of knowledge or arrangements that could help you.

One method for keeping a receptive outlook while posing inquiries is to try not to lead questions.

Driving inquiries are those that are stated in a manner that proposes a specific response or perspective.

All things considered, attempt to pose unconditional inquiries that permit the other individual to give their viewpoint and experiences.

One more method for keeping a receptive outlook while posing inquiries is to listen effectively to the reaction.

Undivided attention includes focusing on what the other individual is talking about, explaining any misconceptions, and considering their reaction prior to giving your own.

Thus, you can acquire a superior comprehension of the point and possibly gain some new useful knowledge.

It's likewise essential to abstain from making presumptions or rushing to make judgment calls while clarifying some things.

All things being equal, move toward each inquiry with interest and a readiness to learn. Assuming you observe that your convictions or presumptions are being tested, attempt to stay liberal and think about elective viewpoints.

posing inquiries is an important instrument for self-awareness and learning.

To keep a receptive outlook while getting clarification on some things, abstain from driving inquiries, listen effectively, try not to make suppositions, and stay inquisitive and liberal.

Thus, you can acquire a more profound comprehension of a theme and possibly find new experiences and arrangements.

Posing incredible inquiries is a craftsmanship that requires practice, persistence, and interest.

By following these tips, you can turn into a more powerful examiner and a superior student. Make sure to be explicit, receptive, aware, and to utilize follow-up questions. With time and practice, you can foster the abilities expected to pose extraordinary inquiries that lead to more profound experiences and more significant discussions.

Chapter Six: Common Pitfalls to Avoid

Posing inquiries is a fundamental piece of correspondence, yet posing the right inquiry in the correct way is difficult all of the time.

Posing some unacceptable inquiry or expressing it improperly can prompt misconceptions, dissatisfaction, and sat around idly. Here are a few normal traps to stay away from while seeking clarification on pressing issues:

A. Asking leading questions

Driving inquiries are questions that are expressed in a manner that recommends a specific response.

These kinds of inquiries can be misdirecting and may not give precise data.

Abstain from posing driving inquiries and on second thought pose unassuming inquiries that permit the respondent to give their own response.

Posing driving inquiries is a method frequently utilized in correspondence, especially in meetings, overviews, and official procedures.

It includes expressing inquiries so that they support or guide the individual being addressed to give a particular kind of reaction.

While driving inquiries can be valuable in specific settings, they can likewise be hazardous whenever utilized improperly.

In this article, we'll investigate the idea of driving inquiries in more detail, examining their likely advantages and disadvantages, as well as offering a few ways to stay away from normal entanglements.

What are Driving Inquiries?

A main inquiry is one that prompts or empowers a specific reaction from the individual being addressed.

For instance, assuming that a legal counselor asks an observer, "Would you concur that the litigant's activities were wild?" This is a main inquiry, as it recommends to the observer that the respondent's activities were, as a matter of fact, foolish.

Driving inquiries can be utilized purposefully or unexpectedly.

At times, they might be utilized as a strategy to impact the reactions of the individual being addressed, while in different cases, they might be the consequence of an unfortunate addressing procedure or absence of readiness.

Advantages of Driving Inquiries

Driving inquiries can be useful in specific settings. For instance, they can be utilized to:

a. Explain data: By posing driving inquiries, a questionnaire can urge an individual to give more point by point or explicit data about a theme.

Brief memory review: While interrogating somebody regarding an occasion, driving inquiries can assist with refreshing their memory and brief them to recall subtleties they could have in any case neglected.

b. Center the discussion: By utilizing driving inquiries, a questionnaire can guide the discussion in a specific bearing, assisting with guaranteeing that important data is covered.

Disadvantages of Driving Inquiries

Notwithstanding their likely advantages, driving inquiries can likewise be dangerous. For instance:

a. They can be intriguing: As we found in the prior illustration of the legal counselor scrutinizing an observer, driving inquiries can propose a specific reaction, possibly driving the individual being addressed to give a response that isn't completely exact or honest.

b. They can lead: By their actual nature, driving inquiries can lead the individual being addressed to a specific reaction, possibly biasing the consequences of a review or interview.

c. They can be manipulative: at times, driving inquiries might be utilized to control the individual being addressed into giving a specific reaction.

This can be especially tricky in legal actions, where the objective is to look for reality.
Ways to stay away from Normal Traps

In the event that you're directing a meeting, review, or legal action, it's critical to know about the likely entanglements of driving inquiries.
 Here are a few ways to keep away from normal slip-ups:

a. Be level headed: Attempt to stay impartial and try not to pose inquiries that propose a specific response. All things considered, expect to pose unassuming inquiries that empower the individual being addressed to give their own point of view.

b. Be ready: Prior to directing a meeting or overview, ensure you've investigated as needed and have a decent comprehension of the subject you're examining somebody regarding.

This will assist you with posing applicable and insightful inquiries that don't depend on driving expressing.

c. Be clear: While seeking clarification on some things, make sure your phrasing is understood and unambiguous.

This will assist with guaranteeing that the individual being addressed comprehends what you're asking and can give a precise reaction.

d. Try not to lead language: Be aware of the language you use while getting clarification on pressing issues.

Try not to utilize words or expressions that recommend a specific response, and on second thought center around nonpartisan language that empowers the individual being addressed to give their own contemplations and feelings.

Driving inquiries can be a helpful device in specific settings, yet they can likewise be dangerous whenever utilized improperly.

By monitoring the likely advantages and disadvantages of driving inquiries, and by following the tips framed in this article, you can guarantee that your scrutinizing strategy is fair, objective, and successful.

B. Asking multiple questions at once

Posing numerous inquiries in a single sentence can befuddle the respondent and make it challenging for them to give a complete response.

To keep away from this, separate your inquiries into individual inquiries, and ask them each in turn.

Posing numerous inquiries on the double is a typical correspondence botch that can prompt disarray and miscommunication.

At the point when we pose a few inquiries in a solitary sentence or message, it tends to be challenging for the beneficiary to comprehend which inquiries to respond to and in what request. This can cause disappointment and could bring about significant data being ignored.

To keep away from this issue, posing each inquiry in turn is ideal.

This permits the beneficiary to zero in on each question separately and give an unmistakable and compact response.

Assuming you have various inquiries, attempt to split them up into discrete messages or sentences to make it more straightforward for the beneficiary to comprehend and answer.

Another significant thought is to make sure your inquiries are understood and explicit.

Unclear or equivocal inquiries can prompt obscure or vague responses, which may not be useful.
Make certain to give sufficient settings and data to assist the beneficiary with seeing

precisely the exact thing you are inquiring about.

it's essential to be aware of the beneficiary's time and consideration.

In the event that you have numerous inquiries, consider whether they are similarly significant and vital.

In the event that a few inquiries can stand by, it could be smarter to focus on the most squeezing ones and ask the others sometime in the future.

Generally, with regards to posing numerous inquiries on the double, toning it down would be ideal.

By asking clear, explicit, and centered questions, you can further develop correspondence and guarantee that your message is perceived and followed up on in the most potentially powerful manner.

C. Using vague language

Confusion and misinterpretation can result from vague wording.

When posing a query, be specific and avoid using unclear language. Ask for clarification or seek a definition if you're unclear about a term.

We can learn important lessons, find solutions to issues, and arrive at wise conclusions by developing the art of asking excellent questions.

It's not always simple to create questions that extract the data we require, though.

The use of ambiguous wording when posing inquiries is a typical error.

This may cause misconceptions and confusion, which eventually prevents us from finding the solutions we're looking for.

We run the danger of our inquiries being misunderstood or misinterpreted when we employ ambiguous language.
For instance, the person we are asking might not be clear on what "this" refers to if we ask them,

"What do you think about this?" Is it a particular notion or suggestion? a broad topic? something totally different? We can avoid misunderstandings and obtain clearer responses by using more precise language.

Vague phrasing might also make our inquiries seem less essential or relevant, which is an issue. If we enquire,

"How do we improve things around here?" It might not be obvious what needs to be improved or why it's crucial.

People might not take the question seriously as a result, or they might lack the desire to provide thoughtful responses.

We can show that we've considered the subject and its importance by being more precise.

So how can we ask questions with more precise language?

Starting by defining precisely what we want to know is one strategy.

We can split the issue down into particular parts, such as "What are the biggest challenges we're facing," rather than asking a broad question like "How can we improve things?"

Alternatively, "What specific improvements would have the biggest impact?"

Another strategy is to make our queries more specific by using examples or scenarios. We can include some context or background information instead of just asking, "What do you think about this idea?" for example, "In light of our recent sales numbers, what do you think about the proposal to focus more on online marketing?"

In the end, being clear and detailed about what we want to know.and making that evident to others is the key to asking effective questions.

We can make sure that our queries are understood, taken seriously, and elicit the information we need to make educated judgments by staying away from ambiguous language and providing concrete examples and scenarios.

D. Assuming you know the answer

Don't pose a question assuming you already know the answer to it. This may impede you from learning new knowledge and result in confirmation bias.

Even if the respondent's response goes against what you had presumptively assumed, have an open mind and be attentive to it.

Assuming you already know the solution has potential drawbacks.

On the one hand, it might give you a sense of assurance and command over a circumstance, but on the other side, it can result in narrow-mindedness, missed learning opportunities, and bad judgment.

When you make the assumption that you already know the solution, you are essentially closing off other options and potential fixes.

This can be especially risky when dealing with complicated or uncharted topics since you might miss important details or solutions that do not conform to your preconceived notions.

Furthermore, assuming you already know the solution can result in overconfidence and arrogance, which can alienate other people and harm your relationships.

Assuming you know everything can make it difficult for you to learn from others or to work effectively, but others value humility and an openness to learning.

A lack of curiosity and a lessened sense of wonder can also result from presuming to know the solution. Assuming you have all the answers can prevent you from fully appreciating the complexity and beauty of the world around you. Life is full of mysteries and surprises.

It's critical to stay open-minded, inquisitive, and humble while yet being confident in your knowledge and skills.

Keep in mind that there is always more to learn and understand, and that believing you know everything can impede your ability to develop and learn.

As a result, if you approach every problem with an open mind and a willingness to learn and consider new options, you might find that you come up with answers and insights that you never would have otherwise.

E. Asking overly complex questions

Asking inquiries that are too complicated or challenging to understand is best avoided. Use straightforward, easy-to-understand language in your queries and keep them simple.

When it comes to effective communication, asking questions that are too complicated might be a typical mistake.

Though it's normal to want to get a lot of information at once, asking questions that are too complicated can actually make things more confusing and difficult to understand.

We will examine possible drawbacks of asking excessively complicated questions in this note and offer advice on how to prevent them.

First off, asking questions that are too complicated can lead to misunderstandings. When faced with a challenging question, people may find it difficult to comprehend what is being asked of them.

This can result in responses that are inaccurate or unrelated to the question at hand.

Complex inquiries can also intimidate and frighten persons who are unfamiliar with the subject, which can further lower the caliber of the solutions offered.

Second, audience engagement may suffer from queries that are too complicated.

People may tune out or lose interest if a question is overly complex, which can reduce communication efficacy. This is especially true when the listener is unfamiliar with the topic or the complexity of the inquiry is superfluous.

Keep your inquiries succinct and precise to minimize these undesirable effects.

By dissecting difficult questions into simpler, more manageable chunks, this can be accomplished.

This can make it simpler for the audience to follow along by ensuring that each component of the question is well understood before going on to the next.

Using basic language and avoiding jargon whenever feasible will also assist to clear up any confusion and increase involvement.

Overly complicated inquiries can impede effective communication by leading to disengagement, misconceptions, and uncertainty. It is crucial to keep questions succinct and clear by segmenting them into smaller, more digestible portions and using plain language whenever possible in order to prevent these undesirable effects.

You may make sure that your audience thoroughly comprehends the material being presented and is able to offer pertinent and accurate comments by doing this.

F. Asking inappropriate or offensive questions

Be aware of the inquiries you pose and try not to pose unseemly or hostile inquiries. This can harm your standing and mischief your relationship with the respondent.

Posing unseemly or hostile inquiries isn't just impolite yet can likewise be terrible and rude.

In the present society, there are sure subjects that are viewed as untouchable, and posing inquiries about them can frequently prompt uneasiness, outrage, or even struggle.

Posing unseemly or hostile inquiries can take many structures. It very well may be posing individual inquiries about somebody's appearance, sexual direction, or orientation character. It very well may be making suspicions in light of somebody's race, religion, or social foundation.

It could likewise be posing inquiries that are excessively personal or excessively testing, like getting some information about somebody's pay, wellbeing status, or family ancestry.

There are many motivations behind why somebody could pose unseemly or hostile inquiries.

It very well may be out of obliviousness, lack of care, or even vindictiveness.

No matter what the inspiration, it's vital to perceive that these kinds of inquiries can adversely affect the individual being asked and can establish an awkward or even threatening climate.

While clarifying some pressing issues, it's critical to consider the unique circumstance and the connection between individuals included.

Assuming you're posing an inquiry of a more odd or a colleague, it's ideal to decide in favor alert and try not to pose individual inquiries that should have been visible as nosy.

In the event that you're posing an inquiry of a companion or a relative, it's essential to be conscious and aware of their limits and solace level.

Assuming you're forced to bear an unseemly or hostile inquiry, it's critical to declare your limits and convey your uneasiness.

You reserve the privilege to define limits and to decline to address questions that make you anxious. You can do this by amiably diverting the discussion, communicating your distress, or just declining to respond to the inquiry.

posing unseemly or hostile inquiries isn't just inconsiderate, yet it can likewise be terrible and rude.

 It's critical to be aware of the effect your inquiries can have on others and to regard their limits and solace level.

 If all else fails, it's smarter to decide in favor alert and try not to pose individual or delicate inquiries. Keep in mind, openness is of the utmost importance, and open and conscious discourse is consistently the best methodology.

G. Interrupting the respondent

Permit the respondent to wrap up addressing your inquiry before you answer. Intruding on them can cause them to feel disregarded and may keep them from giving a total response.

Interfering with a respondent while they are responding to an inquiry should be visible as a rude demonstration that can bring about different adverse results.

Hindering can be because of different reasons, for example, excitement to explain a point, fretfulness, or an absence of listening abilities.

Intruding on the respondent can prompt miscommunication, misconceptions, and even antagonism.

At the point when an individual is intruded on while responding to an inquiry, it can cause them to feel disregarded and insignificant.

It can likewise cause them to feel that their perspective isn't esteemed or that they are not being allowed an opportunity to completely articulate their thoughts.

This can prompt disappointment, and the respondent might become guarded or antagonistic, making it much more challenging to really impart.

Hindering can likewise prompt miscommunication and errors.

At the point when an individual is intruded on, they might misplace their thought process, fail to remember what they planned to say, or give fragmented data. This can bring about a mutilated or erroneous comprehension of the circumstance, prompting wrong choices or activities.

In addition, intruding on the respondent can be seen as an indication of restlessness or an absence of listening abilities.

Interfering with somebody infers that the individual doing the hindering is more worried about making themselves clear than paying attention to the respondent.

This can sabotage the trust and regard that the respondent has for the individual posing the inquiry, making it harder to lay out a decent compatibility and convey really..
.

interfering with the respondent while posing inquiries can have different adverse results, like miscommunication, mistaken assumptions, and aggression. It is vital for extend regard, persistence, and great listening abilities while clarifying some pressing issues and permitting the respondent to completely articulate their thoughts.

This can prompt a superior comprehension of the circumstance and more compelling correspondence, bringing about improved results.

posing inquiries is a basic piece of correspondence, however it's fundamental to keep away from normal traps to guarantee that you get precise and valuable data.

By abstaining from driving inquiries, posing explicit and direct inquiries, and being aware of the respondent's sentiments and reactions, you can further develop your relational abilities and fabricate solid associations with others.

F. Being too aggressive or confrontational

Posing inquiries is a significant piece of correspondence and learning, yet the manner in which we ask them can altogether affect how they are gotten by others.

 Being excessively forceful or fierce while posing inquiries can make strain, aggression, and thwart useful correspondence.

In this note, we will investigate for what reason being excessively forceful or fierce while posing inquiries can be impeding and offer ways to pose inquiries in a more helpful way.

One justification for what reason being excessively forceful or angry while posing inquiries is risky is that it can put the other individual on edge.

At the point when we approach somebody with antagonism, they are bound to feel left behind and answer in kind, as opposed to taking part in a valuable discourse.

This can prompt a breakdown in correspondence and keep us from getting the data we want or accomplishing our ideal result.

Besides, being excessively forceful or fierce while posing inquiries can establish an awkward and threatening climate for other people.

This can deter them from being transparent in their reactions, prompting an absence of trust and genuineness in the relationship.

To stay away from these unfortunate results, moving toward inquiries in a valuable and conscious manner is significant. Here are a few ways to do as such:

a. Begin with a receptive outlook: Prior to posing your inquiry, pause for a minute to think about your tone and approach.

Is it safe to say that you are feeling guarded or antagonistic? Provided that this is true, take a full breath and attempt to relinquish those sentiments.

Move toward the discussion with a receptive outlook and an eagerness to tune in.

b. Utilize an impartial tone: The manner in which you pose your inquiry can immensely affect the way things are gotten.

Utilize an unbiased manner of speaking and try not to utilize accusatory or fierce language. For instance, rather than saying, "For what reason did you do that?" take a stab at saying, "I'm interested about why you decided to do that."

c. Abstain from making suspicions: While posing an inquiry, attempt to try not to make suppositions about the other individual's expectations or inspirations.

All things being equal, center around requesting explanation or more data.

For instance, rather than saying, "You did that intentionally, didn't you?" take a stab at saying, "Could you at any point clarify for me why you settled on that choice?"

d. Be conscious: Regardless of how baffled or irate you might feel, it is vital to stay deferential while seeking clarification on some things.

Stay away from ridiculing, individual assaults, or putting down the other individual. Recall that you are attempting to have a valuable discussion, not a showdown.

being excessively forceful or angry while posing inquiries can strain and thwart useful correspondence.

By moving toward inquiries in a useful and conscious way, we can cultivate a more transparent discourse and accomplish our ideal results all the more successfully.

Make sure to keep a receptive outlook, utilize a nonpartisan tone, try not to make presumptions, and stay conscious, and you will be well en route to improving as a communicator.

Chapter Seven: Summary of key points

This book is a must-peruse for anybody who wishes to further develop their relational abilities and become more viable in their own and proficient lives.

Here are a portion of the central issues that are featured in this book:

a. Questions can open up additional opportunities and open doors:

   The right inquiry can assist us with investigating groundbreaking thoughts, gain experiences, and distinguish valuable open doors that we could have in any case missed.

 By posing extraordinary inquiries, we can grow our reasoning and move toward issues from new points.

b. Incredible inquiries require undivided attention: To pose extraordinary inquiries, we should be great audience members. Undivided attention assists us with understanding what the other individual is talking about, and it empowers us to plan questions that are applicable and interesting.

c. Questions can be utilized to assemble connections: By posing inquiries that show interest in the other individual, we can fabricate compatibility and lay out trust.

At the point when we show that we care about the other individual's considerations and sentiments, we make an association that can prompt further and more significant discussions.

d. Questions can assist us with explaining our reasoning: Posing inquiries can be an amazing asset for self-reflection and self-awareness. By scrutinizing our suspicions and convictions, we can acquire lucidity and knowledge into our own points of view.

e. Incredible inquiries require work on: Posing extraordinary inquiries is an expertise that can be created with training.

By being deliberate about our scrutinizing, and by searching out input and direction, we can turn out to be more viable communicators and better examiners.

Generally, "How to Pose Incredible Inquiries" is a phenomenal asset for any individual who needs to further develop their relational abilities and come out better as an examiner.

By following the standards framed in this book, we can figure out how to pose inquiries that lead to more profound grasping, more significant connections, and better progress in all parts of our lives.

A. Final thoughts on the art of asking thought-provoking questions

The craft of posing intriguing inquiries is a fundamental expertise that can assist people with exploring through life all the more successfully.

Whether you are an understudy, an expert, or just somebody looking for self-improvement, posing the right inquiries can assist you with acquiring a more profound comprehension of yourself and your general surroundings.

At its center, posing provocative inquiries includes testing presumptions, looking for new viewpoints, and investigating the fundamental inspirations driving our activities and convictions. It expects us to step beyond our usual ranges of familiarity and embrace vulnerability, permitting us to defy troublesome issues head-on and pursue more educated choices.

One of the main parts of posing provocative inquiries is figuring out how to effectively tune in.

This implies concentrating entirely on the individual we are talking with, trying to figure out their viewpoint without judgment or assumptions.

Thus, we can foster compassion and assemble more grounded connections, while likewise acquiring significant experiences that can help us in our own lives.

One more key component of posing intriguing inquiries is being willing to pose ourselves intense inquiries. This can be awkward now and again, as it expects us to face our own predispositions and constraints.

In any case, thusly, we can acquire a more clear comprehension of our own qualities and inspirations, permitting us to go with additional deliberate decisions and live additional satisfying lives.

In the present high speed world, it tends to be really quite simple to become involved with the surge of daily existence and neglect to pose ourselves the significant inquiries.

In any case, by finding an opportunity to consider our encounters and search out new points of view, we can acquire a more profound comprehension of ourselves and our general surroundings.

This, thus, can assist us with driving more deliberate and satisfying lives.

the specialty of posing provocative inquiries is an incredible asset for self-improvement and improvement. It expects us to be liberal, compassionate, and able to challenge our own presumptions.

Thus, we can acquire new experiences, fabricate more grounded connections, and lead additional satisfying lives.

Thus, next time you end up in a discussion, pause for a minute to stop and consider what questions you could request to extend your comprehension and flash novel thoughts.

You may be astonished at the bits of knowledge that arise.

Conclusion

All in all, the book "How to ask great questions is an important asset for anybody hoping to work on their scrutinizing abilities.

The book gives keen and viable direction on the most proficient method to pose inquiries that will prompt further figuring out, more useful discussions, and improved results.

One of the vital focal points from the book is the significance of posing unassuming inquiries that welcome insightful reactions.

By keeping away from shut finished questions that can be responded to with a basic "yes" or "no," we can urge others to completely share their considerations and thoughts more.
This, thus, can prompt more innovative and cooperative critical thinking.

The book likewise stresses the worth of undivided attention, which includes giving close consideration to the individual we are talking with and exhibiting that we esteem their feedback.

This not just assists us with bettering their point of view yet additionally shows that we are put resources into the discussion and focused on tracking down a commonly helpful arrangement.

Moreover, the book gives pragmatic counsel on the most proficient method to pose inquiries in various settings, like in gatherings, meetings, and training meetings.

The creator shares explicit procedures for posing testing inquiries, explaining suppositions, and investigating various choices.

Generally speaking, "How to Pose Incredible Inquiries" is a strongly prescribed perused for anybody hoping to further develop their relational abilities.

By figuring out how to pose more compelling inquiries, we can cultivate better connections, improve our critical thinking skills, and make more noteworthy progress in both our own and proficient lives.

Printed in Great Britain
by Amazon

29131054R00106